Other books in the series:
The Crazy World of Birdwatching (Peter Rigby)
The Crazy World of Cats (Bill Stott)
The Crazy World of Golf (Mike Scott)
The Crazy World of Cricket (Bill Stott)
The Crazy World of the Handyman (Roland Fiddy)
The Crazy World of Hospitals (Bill Stott)
The Crazy World of Jogging (David Pye)
The Crazy World of Love (Roland Fiddy)
The Crazy World of Marriage (Bill Stott)
The Crazy World of Music (Bill Stott)
The Crazy World of the Office (Bill Stott)
The Crazy World of Photography (Bill Stott)
The Crazy World of Rugby (Bill Stott)
The Crazy World of Sailing (Peter Rigby)
The Crazy World of the School (Bill Stott)
The Crazy World of Sex (David Pye)
The Crazy World of Skiing (Craig Peterson & Jerry Emerson)
The Crazy World of Tennis (Peter Rigby)

Published in Great Britain in 1987 by
Exley Publications Ltd, 16 Chalk Hill,
Watford, Herts WD1 4BN, United Kingdom.

Copyright © Bill Stott, 1987
Second printing 1988
Third printing 1990
Fourth printing 1991
ISBN 1-85015-079-6

Printed and bound in Hungary.

the
CRAZY
world of
GARDENING

Cartoons by
Bill Stott

EXLEY

"OK you bugs and beetles, weeds and weevils, remember me from last year? Well, I'm back!"

"I merely remarked that we hadn't had a bite all day and he took off like a scalded cat!"

"You chauvinist fork!!"

"See what I mean? You don't just switch these on you know…"

"And do you have to do that even when the fuel switch is off?"

"See? I told you that scarecrow wasn't macho enough!"

"When your mother remodels the garden, she doesn't mess around!"

"If Newton had sat under you, we'd still be waiting for the Theory of Gravity!"

"I don't care where you've come from. You've scorched my lawn!"

"Buy a goat to keep the grass down? Don't be ridiculous! What's that smell...?"

"Grandma's been stung again, Daddy…"

"One of these days I'm going to buy an extension cable and find out how much land I really have..."

"Steve reckons there's this one particular slug..."

"No. I think it was better where we had it in the first place…"

"*Quick! Turn off the water and bring me a knife!*"

"You've decided to tackle the old vegetable patch then?"

"So I said to George, 'We've got the land, we've got the money
– let's have a _real_ rock garden!'"

"No, wait. Let him get a good blaze going before you ring
the fire department..."

"Ah, here it is... 'Sometimes called Throttleweed from the legend
of it being responsible for the disappearance of at least one of
Henry VIII's gardeners...'"

"And that's where I fell off the steps..."

*"That's just typical – he's gone fishing and she's home
with the kids!"*

"Would it hurt so much to clean the bathroom when you've finished?"

"*Working hard, my foot! He's been having a smoke behind the shed!*"

"I take it back! I take it back! Your fingers are greener than mine..."

"... and technically speaking, it's yours!"

"I'm signing him on for Pyromaniacs Anonymous next week…"

"That's Mrs Fisher. She has a sticking throttle…"

"I suppose you don't have a deodorized version, do you?"

"You let him go in there __alone__?!?"

"And your little friends dropped by to help you clean out the shed, did they? How nice!"

"Hello dear! Cousin George dropped by; he's out on the lawn
practising his chip shots..."

"Hi sweetheart, I'm home early. Come and meet our new
Head of Sales..."

"It is the cat! About 10 minutes ago I spilled some of this new fertilizer on it..."

"What do you mean WE called the twins Rosemary and Daisy after what we grew together? If we'd called them after what you'd grown, it would be 'Bored' and 'Blistered'!"

"OK, here they come. You wriggle around, and I'll run
up his leg..."

"So it's true! They <u>can</u> read!!"

"Honey? Have you seen my blue pin-stripe suit – the one you don't like...?"

"It's a tribute to my husband's contribution to this garden..."

"Buzz off!"

"There now – be brave! Real gardeners don't cry when they stick the pitchfork through their foot..."

"I didn't have the heart to tell him face to face..."

"I've been reconsidering. Don't you think pools are getting rather common? Why don't we have a nice rock garden instead?"

"I still think you'd get a better spread with a fork!"

"Let's see the Jones's beat that!"

"No this is 28 Fairdrive Hill. You want 28 Fairhill Drive…"

"Bearing in mind the widely-held theory that plants respond
and flourish when praised, I'm off to insult a few weeds..."

"No, we can't have a fire. You have to <u>grow</u> something before you can have a fire!"

"Evicting him seems a little heartless. After all, you only discovered him because you decided to clean up this section."

"Dandelion colony, bearing 020, behind the hollyhocks..."

"It's a new rose I've developed. It needs a lot of propping up;
I'm thinking of naming it after you."

"We're not speaking. I inadvertently disturbed the gerbil's last resting place while planting out the lettuce!"

"Strange how the mere mention of trimming the hedge gives your back spasms..."

"I'm worried about your dad. He's always talked *to* his plants, but just recently he's started to listen to them as well!"

"The lucky horseshoe fell off the garage wall onto my head. I staggered forward, put the mower into 'drive' inadvertently, thereby destroying the fence. Then it overheated, burst into flames, and really ruined my day!"

"*C'mon son, don't be chicken! I bet I can dig up more seedlings than you can before he spots us...*"

"I still say we're in trouble if the animal protection people
find out..."

"I don't seem to be able to switch it off..."

"Sweetheart! That earring I thought I'd dropped in the compost heap..."

"That's funny. There's a sand wedge and two old putters missing..."

"She hates killing things. She thinks there's a slim chance of insulting the slugs out of the garden."

"Why not eat all of one *leaf*, instead of nibbling them all?"

"*Stop moaning Gloria! I'm not paying good money for a summerhouse and then not use it!*"

"It's not an unexploded bomb; it's an unexploded gas main!"

"What do you expect from a seed called 'Pot Luck'?"

"Of course, the pressure needs a little fine-tuning..."

"You're quite right Sir! It doesn't say anything about having to wear gloves..."

"For heaven's sake, Norman – it's only a mower!"

"Yes, those little blue berries are poisonous!"

"Wouldn't it be easier just to learn their names?"

Books from the "Crazy World" series:

The Crazy World of Birdwatching. £3.99. By Peter Rigby. Over seventy cartoons on the strange antics of the twitcher brigade. One of our most popular pastimes, this will be a natural gift for any birdwatcher.

The Crazy World of Cats. £3.99. By Bill Stott. Fat cats, alley cats, lazy cats, sneaky cats – from the common moggie to the pedigree Persian – you'll find them all in this witty collection. If you've ever wondered what your cat was really up to, this is for you.

The Crazy World of Cricket. £3.99. By Bill Stott. This must be Bill Stott's silliest cartoon collection. It makes an affectionate present for any cricketer who can laugh at himself.

The Crazy World of Golf. £3.99. By Mike Scott. Over seventy hilarious cartoons show the frantic golfer in his (or her) every absurdity. What really goes on out on the course, and the golfer's life when not playing are chronicled in loving detail.

The Crazy World of the Handyman. £3.99. By Roland Fiddy. This book is a must for anyone who has ever hung one length of wallpaper upside down or drilled through an electric cable. A gift for anyone who has ever tried to "do it yourself" and failed!

The Crazy World of Hospitals. £3.99. By Bill Stott. Hilarious cartoons about life in a hospital. A perfect present for a doctor or a nurse – or a patient who needs a bit of fun.

The Crazy World of Love. £3.99. By Roland Fiddy. This funny yet tender collection covers every aspect of love from its first joys to its dying embers. An ideal gift for lovers of all ages to share with each other.

The Crazy World of Marriage. £3.99. By Bill Stott. The battle of the sexes in close-up from the altar to the grave, in public and in private, in and out of bed. See your friends, your enemies (and possibly yourselves?) as never before!

The Crazy World of Music. £3.99. By Bill Stott. This upbeat collection will delight music-lovers of all ages. From Beethoven to Wagner and from star conductor to the humblest orchestra member, no-one escapes Bill Stott's penetrating pen.

The Crazy World of the Office. £3.99. By Bill Stott. Laugh your way through the office jungle with Bill Stott as he observes the idiosyncrasies of bosses, the deviousness of underlings and the goings-on at the Christmas party. . . . A must for anyone who has ever worked in an office.

The Crazy World of Photography. £3.99. By Bill Stott. Everyone who owns a camera, be it a Box Brownie or the latest Pentax, will find something to laugh at in this superb collection. The absurdities of the camera freak will delight your whole family.

The Crazy World of Rugby. £3.99. By Bill Stott. From schoolboy to top international player, no-one who plays or watches rugby will escape Bill Stott's merciless expose of their habits and absurdities. Over seventy hilarious cartoons – a must for addicts.

The Crazy World of Sailing. £3.99. By Peter Rigby. The perfect present for anyone who has ever messed about in boats, gone pea green in a storm or been stuck in the doldrums.

The Crazy World of the School. £3.99. By Bill Stott. A brilliant and hilarious reminder of those chalk throwing days. Wince at Bill Stott's wickedly funny new collection of crazy school capers.

The Crazy World of Sex. £3.99. By David Pye. A light-hearted look at the absurdities and weaker moments of human passion – the turn-ons and the turn-offs. Very funny and in (reasonably) good taste.

The Crazy World of Skiing. £3.99. By Craig Peterson and Jerry Emerson. Covering almost every possible (and impossible) experience on the slopes, this is an ideal present for anyone who has ever strapped on skis – and instantly fallen over.

The Crazy World of Tennis. £3.99. By Peter Rigby. Would-be Stephen Edbergs and Steffi Grafs watch out! This brilliant collection will pin-point their pretensions and poses. Whether you play by yourself or only watch TV, this will amuse and entertain you!

These books make super presents. Order them from your local bookseller or from Exley Publications Ltd, Dept BP, 16 Chalk Hill, Watford, Herts WD1 4BN. (Please send £1.50 for one book or £2.25 for two or more to cover postage and packing.)